# THE GOLDENDOODLE GUIDE

The ultimate handbook for new and prospective owners. Training, raising and caring for your goldendoodle.

Anthony Portokaloglou

Disclaimer Notice

The techniques described in this book are for informational purposes only. All attempts have been made by the author to provide real and accurate content. No responsibility will be taken by the author for any damages cost by misuse of the content described in this book. Please consult a licensed professional before utilizing the information of this book.

Thank you for choosing this book. I hope you will find this book useful. Please could you leave a review on the website where you bought the book!

# INTRODUCTION- MEET THE GOLDENDOODLE

The Goldendoodle is an amazing breed. The Goldendoodle breed is a purposefully bred hybrid that is often called a "designer dog". Goldendoodle is the result of breeding Golden Doodles with Poodles. They are highly recommended for families, are equally great for singles, and are a long-term companion. They are known for their pleasant personalities and loyalty, and they are also very smart, sometimes almost too smart. **Both of their parent breeds are in the list of top five trainable dogs**.

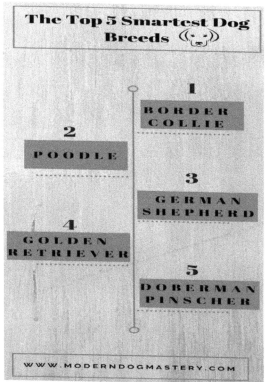

Although technically they are not considered a breed of their own, there are some efforts being made to change that. Even if you are looking for a purebred dog, don't overlook the

6

Goldendoodle as an option. This dog is the best of two lines of pure breeds. In the past having to make a choice between dog breeds could be very difficult; in this case both the Golden Doodle and the Standard Poodle have many great traits.

Often sought for their hybrid and hypoallergenic qualities, it is important to note that although many are truly hypoallergenic, some Goldendoodles have been found to shed, although very minimally. They best fit with people who are allergic to dogs.

Seek an experienced, reputable, and educated breeder. There are genetic factors to consider for the health of the future puppies. If a reputable breeder has done it correctly then what is produced is likely one of the most lovable and intelligent dogs. These dogs embody the best qualities of both of their parent lines and are very easy to train.

Of course, it may sound too good to be true, but remember, a dog is still a product of its environment and how it is raised. Bringing home, a Goldendoodle puppy won't magically give you the perfect pet, but having the right environment and consistent training, can. Although Goldendoodles do not need extensive exercise, they are still a large breed, so you will need to make sure that your home is suitable, and the amount of time you have to devote to the puppy is suitable. Goldendoodles love people and must be kept indoors. A Goldendoodle does best in a house, especially if there is a yard that it can roam in. For those that live in apartments but are still hoping for the joy and companionship of a Goldendoodle you can look into the option of a Miniature Goldendoodle whose size is more suited for apartment living.

There are a few additional things to consider before deciding to welcome a Goldendoodle into your home and family. The Goldendoodle's beautiful coat requires fairly extensive care, unless it is cut short and groomed every six to eight weeks. If you want your doodle to have a longer coat, be prepared to brush them on a daily basis.

Goldendoodle is a large breed and therefore will require a bit more attention when it comes to training and exercise. Although Goldendoodles are fantastic swimmers, their agility should also not be overlooked. With these qualities Goldendoodles do very well with people who live an active outdoor lifestyle, however they will also do just fine curled up in the living room. They are very amiable dogs, and usually will get along with other animals and children. If you do decide to bring a Goldendoodle home, make sure you have a crate for crate training, as well as some chew toys. You're best off purchasing non-spill food and water bowls, as Goldendoodles can get enthusiastic when they eat.

# CHAPTER 1: THINGS TO KNOW BEFORE GETTING A GOLDENDOODLE

## HOW TO CHOOSE THE BEST GOLDENDOODLE FOR YOU

You have made the first step. You decided you want a Goldendoodle. Next step is to decide what type of Goldendoodle. Well, it depends on many factors such as the size. Maybe you want a smaller dog if you have kids. Or you prefer a larger dog. Some other people prefer a dog somewhere in the middle. The good news is that all sizes are available when choosing a goldendoodle. In order to decide which is the ideal Goldendoodle for you, you need to check as much information as possible. Your options are not limited only in size but also in coat type and color.

**Goldendoodle coat colors** are: white, cream, apricot, gold, red, and rarely gray and black which are also called Phantom Goldendoodle.

**Goldendoodle Height:** Vary from 13 to 24 (33.2 – 60.96 cm) inches at the shoulder depending on Poodle parent which can be a miniature or a standard poodle.

**Weight:** miniature Goldendoodle: 15 to 30 pounds (6.8 to 13.6 Kg); medium Goldendoodle: 30 to 45 pounds (13.6 to 20.4 Kg) and standard Goldendoodle 45 (20.4 Kg) to more than 100 pounds (45.35Kg).

Below are the different types of Goldendoodle:

## F1 Goldendoodles

The first generation Goldendoodles is identified with the code F1. These Goldendoodles are the result of pure Poodle and Golden Retriever. As you expect the product of this breeding is 50% poodle and 50% Golden Retriever. F1 Goldendoodles are the traditional Doodle that many people think of a Goldendoodle. These dogs are intelligence, loving and hypoallergenic. They still shed but not that much. Their coat is long and curly.

## F1B Goldendoodles

F1B generation Doodle is a product of cross-breed a F1 Doodle with a Poodle. The F1B Goldendoodle will be 75% Poodle and 25% Retriever. This generation is more popular due to the non-shedding characteristics that occurs 99% of the time. The F1B generation is the most hypoallergenic of the different generations and that's why this type is the best if you have severe allergies. Fortunately, the F1B has the same strength, good health and the favorable personality characteristics. Their coat type can be long and wavy or shorty and curly. Lastly with F1B generations you can find more color variation.

## F2 Goldendoodles

F2 is the second generation of Goldendoodles. F2 have both parents F1 Doodles. With F2 type you can get equal amounts of Doodle and Poodle. The F2 Doodles characteristics are similar to the F1 Doodles. Most likely you will get light shedding with this generation Goldendoodle. F2 are good for homes with light allergies.

## F2B Doodles – Multigenerational Doodles

F2B is a mix of generations such as F1 Doodle and an F1B Doodle. This is great generation with non-shedding quality. It is excellent for people with moderate allergies. With F2B you still get the good traits of personality as well as good health.

# MALE VS FEMALE DOGS

'Male vs female dogs'. What are the real differences? We look at the pros and cons of choosing a male or a female goldendoodle. As soon as you find a good breeder, the next step is to decide between male and female dog.

Here are some tips.

When they are puppies there is slight difference between a boy and a girl. Males can be slightly larger than females. However, puppies grow up fast and they have differences when they reach maturity.

Male dogs are usually a little larger (taller and heavier) than females dogs. Boys have different look as well. They look more masculine with bigger heads.

If dog is not neutered, then female dogs come on heat for three to four weeks twice a year and during this period you cannot walk with your dog in public places since they have a bloody vaginal discharge. And most likely you don't want them on your pale carpets and furniture.

In case you decide to spray your female goldendoodle then the operation is expensive and is not covered by pet insurance.

Once a non-neutered male goldendoodle reaches sexually mature age, he will 'roam' in order to find a mate. Females may roam as well but roaming is more common for boys. All you need to do when you have a male dog is to use a dog proof perimeter around your yard.

Another main concern of new dog owner is that males are more aggressive. Based on studies male dogs are more likely to bite than female dogs. However, this is not a clear cut since there are many reasons to take into account why a dog bite. For example, it could be that more people were bitten from male dogs because male dogs as aforementioned roam more to find a mate.

Male dogs predominate in sports and this is an indication that they can be trained easier. But again, here we need to check out the facts. Usually in competitive sports dogs are purebred and they are rarely spayed. So, females don't usually attend these kind of sports because they might be tied up with pregnancy or lactation.

Lastly differences between a boy and a girl goldendoodle are very few.

If you prefer females, then go for a female dog. And vice versa.


BEST 16 FACTS ABOUT GOLDENDOODLE:

1. Goldendoodle are the best choice for people with allergies.

2. They are very intelligent dogs and the reason is that they are the product of cross breeding smart dogs. (golden retriever and poodles).

3. Goldendoodles have multiple names: Of course, goldendoodle is the most common one. Other names are 'Golden Poos,' 'Groodles' and 'Goldie Poos.'

4. They are considered a new dog breed and their origin is North America and Australia.

5. Natural vigorous: They are hybrid vigor and they are healthier than their parents. (golden retriever and poodles).

6. Grooming bills are minimal. Just wash their fur occasionally (monthly) and comp to make it shiny.

Goldendoodles need trimming since their hair grows.

7. They are a great companion for older adults, sick people and children. They are lovable and social pets.

8. They are eager to learn new tricks and commands and they like to be continually brain stimulated.

9. They are great guide and therapy dogs. Goldendoodles are obedient, loyal, loving and funny. So, they act as therapy dogs for blind people, hospital patients, elderly people and people in nursing homes.

10. Goldendoodles vary in colour like white, black, golden, orange, dark brown and grey. Their coat is silky and the hair can be curly or straight.

11. No two Goldendoodles are alike. Because Goldendoodles are not purebreds their characteristics cannot be predicted.

12. Goldendoodles have different kind of dog types.

Toy Goldendoodle

Teacup Goldendoodle

Micro Goldendoodle

Tiny Goldendoodle

Giant Goldendoodle

# DO YOU NEED A LICENSE?

Dog licensing regulations vary depending on your region. There aren't really any federal laws regarding this, as this is more of a local matter. The best way to check whether you will need to secure a license for your dog is to check with your local legislature or council to determine what requirements prevail in your area.

Even if you are not legally required to get a license, however, it might be a good idea to do so voluntarily anyway. This way, your ownership is legally registered, and it will be easier for other people to trace your dog back to you in case he ever gets lost. It will also be a good way to assert your ownership over your Goldendoodle in case such a situation ever arises.

Licenses in general are only granted after the payment of a small fee, and proof of rabies vaccination. Since you should have your dog vaccinated against rabies anyway, this isn't really a troublesome requirement. Licenses are usually renewable on an annual basis, during which time you should again provide proof of revaccination. This tells us that licensing is intended not only to regulate ownership, but also to protect both your dog and the public against rabies. Again, check your local laws to verify the specific requirements prevailing in your region.

## HOW MANY GOLDENDOODLES SHOULD YOU KEEP?

The decision to keep more than one Goldendoodle is a personal one, and each person will have to make this decision based on his or her unique circumstances. Perhaps the only thing that need to be said on this score is that you should only keep more than one Goldendoodle if you are sure that you can afford their upkeep, including food, grooming, medical expenses, and also have the time and energy to socialize, exercise, groom and train with both dogs on a regular basis.

As you will see later in this chapter, keeping one dog can easily translate to a substantial yearly cost, and keeping more than one dog will easily translate to at least double this basic amount. And taking care of any dog requires energy commitment that a full time working person may not be able to spare. The main consideration you should have on keeping more than one Goldendoodle is whether or not this is for the best interests of the dog. If doing so will mean that you will not be able to provide fully for each of them, or that it is beyond your financial capacity, then the answer is probably no.

If you can afford it easily, however, without any detrimental effect on your own expenses, and if you have the room, the time and the energy for it, then certainly having more than one Goldendoodle in the house can be a very rewarding and enjoyable experience. This is a very loving, affectionate and intelligent breed, and having more than one to keep you - and each other - company, can be worthwhile.

## DO GOLDENDOODLES GET ALONG WITH OTHER PETS?

Goldendoodles are a generally friendly breed. Provided there was proper socialization training in his early months and years, Goldendoodles can be quite popular and well-loved by other pets, by your other family members, by the neighbors, and even by strangers!

Yes, this is a sociable breed, and they are just as likely to wag their tail at strangers coming to your door rather than bark a warning. They will also prove to be loyal and affectionate companions to other pets, whether it be another dog, another Goldendoodle, or even cats! Just make sure that you properly supervise the introductory meetings between your Goldendoodle and other pets.

If you keep other smaller pets, such as birds or mice, for instance, it is probably best to exercise before, since Goldendoodles have a hunting instinct.

## HOW MUCH DOES IT COST TO KEEP A GOLDENDOODLE?

Finally, let's talk numbers. One of the things you'll probably notice during the process of adoption or purchase of a Goldendoodle puppy is a series of questions regarding your lifestyle, your home situation, and your financial situation. This is because breeders and those who work at finding homes for rescues know that the costs of keeping a pet can add up. Aside from various dog equipment and accessories, there is also the annual cost of food, medical expenses, vaccinations, and grooming. All these are necessary for your dog to live a long, healthy and fulfilling life, and any person interested in keeping a Goldendoodle should be able to show that they can afford the yearly costs.

How much, do you wonder, does keeping a Goldendoodle cost?

Your expenses will necessarily be larger during the first year, as there will be one-time initial expenses such as the cost of purchase or adoption (the purchase price of a Goldendoodle puppy can range from around $1,400 to as high as $3,000), spaying and/or neutering ($90-200), vaccinations ($80-300), and the cost of various pet equipment and accessories such as food and water bowls, a dog bed, a leash and harness ($250-500).

# Initial Costs of Keeping a Goldendoodle

| Purchase Price | $1,400-3,000 (around $250-300 for adoptions) |
|---|---|
| Spaying or Neutering | $90-200 |
| Vaccinations | $80-300 |
| Dog Accessories and Equipment | $250-500 |

All this is apart from the annual recurring costs of food, medical checkups, grooming, and even training costs. Below you will find a general estimate of some of the annual expenses that you can expect to cut into your budget. Please take note that these are only general ballpark figures, and are adjustable depending on the price ranges in your area of products and services.

## Annual Expenses for Keeping a Goldendoodle

| | |
|---|---|
| Dog Food | $150-500 |
| Veterinary/Medical Costs | $160-670 |
| Supplies | $150-1,700 |
| Training | $30-500 |
| Grooming Costs | $20-400 |
| Miscellaneous Yearly Expenses (licenses, boarding, etc.) | $100-500 |

Of course, having a pet as lovable as a Goldendoodle is not just an investment of money, but also of love. For some people, having a pet in the house to help them de-stress, provide loyal and loving companionship, and even a kind of psychological security might actually translate to savings in terms of their own medical costs. Keeping a pet can help lower your stress levels, keep depression at bay, and can also keep a person healthier physically, mentally, and emotionally.

# WHAT ARE THE PROS AND CONS OF GOLDENDOODLES?

Still on the fence about getting a Goldendoodle? Perhaps the high purchase price is making you have second thoughts. One of the best ways to determine whether or not a Goldendoodle is the right dog for you is to have a brief overview of the pros and cons of keeping a dog, and a Goldendoodle in particular. This will allow you to keep the big picture in mind as you attempt to make up your mind on whether or not it is feasible for you to add a Goldendoodle to your home situation.

**Pros for the Goldendoodle Breed**

- A fairly predictable temperament in comparison with other mixed designer dog hybrids. This is an affectionate, friendly crossbreed, playful, and even goofy at times. They make great family pets.

- If you find the right dog that can be trained to serve as an aid dog, and with a hypo-allergenic coat to boot (take note that not all Goldendoodles may fit this profile!), it is a priceless combination of the best of two purebred dog qualities

- Goldendoodles live for a fairly long time, which means that that initial investment of a purchase price can be worth the companion of a lifetime

- This is an intelligent breed, fairly easy to train, and eager to please their human families. Both Poodles and Golden Doodles have a long history of great camaraderie and loyal devotion to their human families.

## Cons for the Goldendoodle Breed

- Goldendoodles can be fairly high maintenance in terms of grooming - aside from regular brushing, you will probably also have to pay a visit to a professional groomers every couple of months or so.

- Goldendoodles, as a breed, are unfortunately at risk of contracting a great number of health conditions or diseases - congenital traits from both Golden Retriever and Poodle breeds. The risk can be minimized through responsible breeding programs and a battery of health checks, but the possibility of a wide range of illnesses will still be there.

- Goldendoodles are not always hypo-allergenic, which means they are not always a feasible choice for people suffering with allergies. And because of the varying results of crossbreeding while this breed is still relatively new, even puppies with hypo-allergenic coats may not always be temperamentally suited to being guide dogs. There is still an element of uncertainty and unpredictability in the kind of Goldendoodle you will be getting (as opposed to the predictability of purebreds)

- This is an expensive breed, which in itself might be off-putting to some.

- Goldendoodles are not recognized by any international dog organization or association. Being a relatively new crossbreed, there is much that is still unknown about Goldendoodles, which consequently decreases the factor of predictability in what you are getting with one of these dogs.

# FOUR HIGH IMPORTANT QUESTION TO ASK THE GOLDENDOODLE BREEDER

Finding a quality Goldendoodle breeder can be difficult since many people are breeding this kind just for profit however there are a lot of quality breeders. Avoiding bad breeders can be easy if you know what to ask them. The more questions you ask the better.

Below are some basic questions you should ask a breeder:

1. Could you show me where you raise the dogs? If the breeder refuses to show you then look elsewhere.

2. Can you show me his/her parents? Again, if the answer is 'no' then stop dealing with this breeder.

3. Can you tell me who your Vet is? Same as above. Red flag if answer is negative.

4. Why there are so many different litters available? Usually most of the breeders have 1 or 2 per year. If breeder has e.x 5 liters at the same time then most probably he/she is running a puppy mill.

BEST TIPS FOR WORKING GOLDENDOODLES OWNERS:

The ideal scenario is spending all day with our dogs. But the reality is that most of us work full time. It is an undeniable fact that working dog owners can result to neglected dogs.

Fortunately working full time and raising a Goldendoodle can be done. Your main concern as a puppy owner is to make sure that your dog is safe and healthy while you are at work.

Some basic tips:

1. Puppies cannot stay alone for a long period of time. The number of hours they can stay alone depends on the dog's age. They need companionship, four meals a day and last but not least potty training. If puppy is around 8-10 weeks old then he needs a lot of attention. It is best to take some days off and spent it with him or hire someone to help you.

2. Consider keeping the dog in a large area with access to puppy pads in case the puppy is alone for more than the period he is capable of holding 'it'.

3. Goldendoodles puppies are chewers. They can chew anything for instance a table's legs or even the floor cover. You will need a puppy proof area. For extreme chewers consider buying a puppy pen and barriers so that the area which your puppy has access is controlled.

4. Puppies usually feel lonely and they often howl and bark/scream. Your neighbors will hear it and they won't like it. In order to manage separation anxiety, you can provide entertainment such as leaving the radio or tv on or even leaving a piece of cloth with your scent.

5. Loneliness for a puppy can be very stressful. Consider taking some days off from your job and train your goldendoodle how to be alone without you. This training process should be done gradually. Your puppy will howl and bark less.

6. Consider installing a pet monitoring system in order to know at any time that your puppy is fine at home. Some special cameras have also 2-way microphone so you can talk to your goldendoodle.

7. Another way to help your puppy not to feel lonely while you are at work is to give him toys or things that can get him busy such as "Kong" type of toy or other treat dispensing toys.

8. As an alternative solution you can look for a daycare service. In these special places your dog can be socialized and trained from an expert. But the best part is that he will go back home exhausted.

9. As an alternative option would be to check if you would be allowed to bring your new goldendoodle puppy at work.

# CHAPTER 2: TAKING CARE OF YOUR GOLDENDOODLE

Essential Basic Care for Your New Goldendoodle

Learning how to care for your Golden Doodle starting as soon as he is a puppy really helps you to mitigate future health problems that he may have. Feeding, grooming, and exercising your Doodle properly is essential for each phase of his life. You want to take him to the vet regularly as per his instructions. Oh, and be warned at visit, chances are he'll resist it. Lastly keeping him mentally and physically active throughout his life, will help him to minimize behaviors issues.

## FEEDING

Canine nutrition is incredibly important for your dog's wellbeing. His nutritional needs will depend on his age, activity level, and breed. Make sure to pick the proper food for your dog. Below a piece of advice on how to feed your dog, and what types of food you should choose.

## Dry Food

When picking a dry food, ensure that the ingredient is real meat. Don't pick up a brand that lists something like corn meal or wheat first. Also avoid words like by-product, animal, and 'meat', as these are terms for ground-up animal parts left over at the meat packing facilities. You want to find foods that contain things like real beef, and real chicken, beef meal or chicken meal because it means that there is more actual meat present in the food. Also, try to select a dog food that offers a rich selection of vitamins and minerals.

There are dry foods specifically formulated for puppies, seniors, obese dogs, diabetic dogs, active dogs, large breeds, small breeds, etc. Be sure to pick a type of dog food that matches what your Goldendoodle will need according to his health, weight and age.

## Wet Food

A wet dog food diet can be useful for dogs who suffer from constipation. You can also feed wet food in combination with dry or raw food. Be careful with wet food, as it can cause diarrhea in your pup. Choose a wet food that contains primarily meat. Look for canned foods with lots of vitamins and minerals. Remember always, that your Goldendoodle has an entirely different digestive system than we humans. It is best to never feed your dog from your table, or while you are yourself snacking. And this can be easily avoided by changing the natural begging behavioral habits while training your Goldendoodle. (No begging = less guilt and more enjoyable snack times for you and your family or guests.)

## Raw Food

A raw food diet can be great for your Goldendoodle since it more closely mimics what he would eat on his own in the wild. However, you have to take care to avoid feeding your dog contaminated food. A good rule of thumb is to avoid feeding your Goldendoodle anything you wouldn't eat. Stick to human standards for safe food.

You can freeze meat and thaw it for your dog, or you can buy raw food mixes that are already prepared. The raw food needs to have more meat than any other ingredient. Dogs like veggies, though, so be sure to include things like peas and carrots. We will talk about what not to feed your dog in a minute.

## How Much to Feed your Goldendoodle

How much you feed your dog depends on his stamina, age, activity level, and breed. You can gauge if you should feed your dog more based on whether or not you can feel his ribs. If his ribs don't stick out, you know that you are feeding enough. If his ribs become covered in fat, you need to cut back on food.

## When to Feed Fido

You should not wean your puppy from his mom until he is about eight weeks old. To grow properly, he needs his mother's milk during the first eight weeks of his life. Only after eight weeks can you begin to feed him real dog food.

Puppies need to eat three to four times a day. Establish a consistent feeding schedule. Avoid feeding your puppy too close to bedtime, or he will have to go potty while you are trying to sleep, and he may mess in the house if you don't let him out quickly enough. No one wants that, right? It is a good idea to split the puppy's daily feeding portion into thirds or fourths and feed him at regular times each day. For puppies, be sure to feed him only puppy food to give him the nutrients he needs to grow into an adult dog. Soak dry puppy food in hot water to make it easier for him to eat and digest.

As your Goldendoudle enters adulthood, you can cut down to feeding twice a day as you make the switch to adult dog food. A consistent routine is beneficial for your dog's mental well-being and sense of calm. It is best feeding at seven in the morning and then five at night. Some dogs are content eating on the same bowl of food all day, so one feeding is all that is necessary. Other dogs like to wolf down their food, especially if they feel competition from other dogs that you may have in the home, so be sure to feed these gluttons twice a day. Simply split the daily feeding portion in half and feed twice. You don't want to overfeed your dog, even if he wolfs his food down and acts hungry for the rest of the day. Don't let him con you. His daily recommended nutritional portion is a good guideline for how much to feed him.

One big part of dog ownership is establishing that you are the alpha dog in the pack. This means that you get to eat first. Your dog must wait patiently until you finish your food and clear the table. Only then should you feed him. Doing this establishes your dominance and teaches your dog that he does not rule the roost. He may need to go into his crate during your meal times if he is too rowdy with the begging for table scraps.

Switching Foods

To switch food brands, try this switching schedule:

- Day 1-2 Mix ¼ new with ¾ old foods

- Day 2-4 Mix ½ new with ½ old

- Day 5-6 Mix ¾ new with ¼ old

- Day 7 100% of the new dog food

When switching your puppy to adult food, you should start at about nine to twelve months for small breeds, twelve months for medium breeds, and twelve to twenty-four months for large breeds. Use the switching schedule above to introduce your dog to the new adult food. Usually it is best to stick to the same brand of adult food as the puppy food that you fed Fido, but you can switch if you find a healthier brand.

Healthy Treats and Snacks

Here are some healthy human foods you can offer your dog in his diet or as treats:

- Oatmeal

- Yogurt

- Apples with the seeds removed

- Peanut butter

- Cheese

- Bananas

- Beef jerky or other jerkies

- Meat, cooked or raw after being properly frozen

- Berries

- Melons

- Green beans. Be careful, as this can act as a laxative for your dog.

- Peas

- Squash and pumpkin

- Brewer's yeast. Not baker's yeast, which can make your dog very sick.

- Carrots

- Eggs

- Salmon or other fish

Foods to Avoid at all Costs

I have touched on this above, but it's important to devote a section to the following: You probably know that dogs are different from humans. Some foods that we can eat with no problem can be toxic to dogs. Here is some of the food you should always avoid:

•	Table scraps. Feeding your dog table scraps teaches him to beg. It also makes him feel entitled to your food. Finally, you don't always know what is in your food and you may feed your dog something that makes him sick.

•	Onion or garlic

•	Chocolate. Especially dark chocolate

•	Grapes or raisins

•	Macadamia nuts

•	Fruit pits or seeds

•	Soft bones such as from pork or poultry

•	Potato peelings or green potatoes

•	Rhubarb leaves

•	Yeast dough or baker's yeast

•	Human vitamins or medications

- Broccoli

- Caffeine

- Alcohol

- Mushrooms

- Persimmons

- Avocadoes

- Raw egg. Can give your dog salmonella poisoning

- Xylitol which can be found in foods such as brand named peanut butters

## EXERCISING YOUR GOLDENDOODLE

Exercise is essential to any dog's health. Just like people, dogs need exercise to stay healthy. A sedentary dog is prone to obesity, muscle problems, diabetes, and heart problems as he gets older. On top of that, a lack of exercise can create a bored dog, which in turn can create an unruly dog. You want to keep your dog occupied with plenty of fun, free play outside and with exercise.

The average dog requires thirty minutes to two hours of physical activity a day. You can provide some of this activity just by letting him run around in a yard. But some of this activity you need to be proactive about. Play fetch or Frisbee to get him running. Take him on walks. Go for hikes together. This physical activity has the added benefit of getting you out and moving too.

## GROOMING

Grooming your dog's hair is an important and sometimes challenging task.

**Brushing**

You should brush your dog's hair at least once a week (longer coat doodles might need daily grooming). Goldendoodles have thick, luscious coats that require care. So be sure to stick to this schedule as needed.

Have your Goldendoodle standing on all fours or lying down comfortably. Fussier dogs may need to lay down so that you can straddle them. Use a slicker brush first. Then use a long-tooth under rake to get deeper into your dog's coat.

Provide trimming or get professional grooming as needed. Dogs with thicker coats will need more trimming and grooming, especially in the hotter months. It's a good idea to let their hair grow thicker during the colder months in your region.

## Bathing

You may be tempted to bath your new best friend often, but keep in mind that his natural oils keep his skin and hair healthy. Too much washing can strip those oils away. Therefore, it is best to bathe your Goldendoodle only once a month.

Make sure to buy a quality dog shampoo such as Earth Bath Shampoo and a slip-resistant mat for those "everyone gets wet shaky moments". Also have a hair dryer and three or four thick towels within easy reach. You want to wear clothes that you don't mind getting wet, and perhaps a little stinky too.

1.    Lay down the slip-resistant mat nearby your tub for safety and comfortability

2.    Now gently ease your Goldendoodle into the bathtub. Dogs usually resist baths until they are used to the process. Be sure to make him feel relaxed by offering lots of praise and a treats.

3. Once your Goldendoodle is in the bathtub, you can start running the water. Before soaking your dog, test the water temperature with your fingers carefully. Make sure that it is comfortable, luke warm water.

4. Get your dog's entire body wet and begin rubbing in the shampoo to create a gentle lather. Don't use so much that you can't rinse it all out, but also don't use so little that you can't create a rich lather. Try your best to avoid his eyes and mouth. Rinse face often as necessary during bathing.

5. Trick: Bathe his head last. This is the part that he will shake and get shampoo all over you, the floor, the walls, and well, you get the picture

6. Now rinse him thoroughly using lukewarm water. Gently work the shampoo out with your hands from top to bottom. Do this several times to get all of the shampoo out so his natural oils can get busy keeping him healthy

7. Now turn the water off and wrap him in a towel. Rub him down thoroughly. You can use a hair dryer after this to effectively dry his entire body. Caution: NEVER USE A HOT SETTING WHEN USING A BLOW DRYER! Place the setting on cool or warm and

test it 6 inches from your bare skin on your inner side wrist. If you can hold it there indefinitely, so will your dog feel comfortable while keeping him happy and from harm.

## Nails

Your Goldendoodle needs his nails to grip, scratch and dig. Be sure to keep your dog's nails relatively short to prevent him from scratching you or injuring himself. If your dog's nails become resistant, you can have your local dog groomer or veterinarian do this for you at a nominal rate. Or you can do it yourself if your dog cooperates. You should buy a pair of special dog nail clippers.

1.   Hold your dog between your legs if he is small, or if larger, have him stand.

2.   Pick up each foot with your hand, so it bends naturally and comfortably. Trim each dog nail separately and delicately, taking your time on each. You never want to hit his quick, which is inside the dog's nail which contains blood vessels and sensitive nerve endings. Focus on the furthest end from the paw, the most translucent part of his nail that you can see through when you hold a light to his paw.

3.    Dogs with white nails will have obvious quicks, which are pink and darker and thicker than the rest of his nail. Goldendoodles can have white nails but are more likely to have black or a combination of black and white.

4.    In black nails that you can't see the quick, trim little pieces of the horn of his nail. Then inspect the nail to see if there is bleeding. Do it a bit at a time and be patient. You never want to hit the quick or you will cause your Goldendoodle pain and as a result, a bad association with nail trimming.

5.    File the end to a smooth, round surface with a regular emery board.

6.    Consider a smoothing oil, like coconut oil, to soften his paws. Use beeswax to heal cracks.

## Your Goldendoodle's Teeth

Try to brush his teeth at least four times a week to prevent gum disease and other dental issues. You can buy a special dog toothbrush and toothpaste which should be meat or poultry-flavored. Start first by getting him comfortable with the notion and goal that it's a good thing.

1. Put a dab on your finger and let him smell it and lick it to get him comfortable.

2. Then try inserting your finger into his mouth and rubbing his gums gently and without too much force.

3. Soon he'll get used to this without too much resistance. When he lets you do this without freaking out, you can try using the dog tooth brush.

4. Use gentle but firm strokes to get his gums and all of his teeth. It won't be perfect, but the idea is to get most of his dental surface area covered in the foam of the toothpaste.

5. There is no need to rinse. He will swallow the toothpaste without problems. However, try to encourage him to drink from his water bowl after a brushing.

Also, keep plenty of stimulating toys with nibs and dental chews around for your dog. These treats will keep him occupied mentally while also keeping his teeth clean and his gums strong and healthy.

## Eyes

Check your dog's eyes regularly to make sure he has no irritation, bleeding, or swelling. Use a cotton ball dipped in warm water to clean away debris and eye boogers whenever you brush him.

## Anal Sacs

My Favorite section. We all know about the infamous anal sac. If not, you will become familiar soon enough. Fact, It's one of the great wonders of dog ownership. If your Dog smells bad or is frequently licking and scooting his bum on your carpets, you know that it's time to expunge the fluid in his anal sacs. Both female and male dogs have anal sacs that can become impacted at any age, so you will have to do this with any dog. The anal sacs are located directly beneath the skin around his anal muscles. Ready to Expunge? Here's How:

1.    Don a pair of plastic or rubber gloves.

2.    Put your dog in a bathtub. This can get messy.

3.    Rub gently upward and inward, pressing the glands toward his anus. Like a teenager's zit on prom night.

4.    The fluid should ooze out of his anus. It should be a brown, strong-smelling oil. If nothing comes out, you may want to take him to the vet to investigate.

# CHAPTER 3: TRAINING YOUR GOLDENDOODLE

After your dog has adjusted to your home, you can officially begin training him. Although you might have started to train him by introducing him to his sleeping area and potty area, you might need to reinforce for the following few weeks until he becomes fully trained.

You're in luck, however, because the Goldendoodle is one of the most intelligent breeds of dogs, so you won't have too much of a hard time. In fact, I think you'll find your training sessions with your dog very enjoyable.

This chapter covers the basics of training that you need to do with your Goldendoodle to ensure that it stays well-behaved and playful instead of bored and destructive.

## Working With Your Training Style

Dog trainers often vary their training styles depending on a dog's temperament and breed, as well as the type of training that the dog needs to undergo. However, despite disagreement and controversies about what training is best for Goldendoodles and other breeds, there is a general consensus about which training styles are best if you want your dog to learn quickly.

Here are some training styles you can consider for your Dood. These dogs' combined intelligence and temperament make them excellent trainees.

1. Positive reinforcement (R+)

This training style is the most recommended by professional trainers. Positive reinforcement entails setting up a rewards system not only for every behavior or trick learned, but also for good behavior in general.

During puppyhood, Goldendoodle training shouldn't take more than five to 10 minutes. Any longer than that and the puppy will become unable to concentrate. Plus they will get too tired to do any other activity. Also, puppies are more easily distracted than older dogs, so that's another hurdle you'd face if you conduct training sessions longer than the time recommended.

R+ training doesn't recommend the use of physical punishment to admonish negative behavior. Instead, they simply withdraw attention from the Goldendoodle by completely ignoring them.

Negative response or attention (such as pushing away the dog in cases of jumping) to your pet's misbehavior is still often interpreted as a form of attention, so it won't really curb his negative behavior. Withdrawing attention is a good way to gain your dog's attention, and makes him more amenable for further training.

2. Operant conditioning

This training style is the basis of positive reinforcement. Conditioning is a psychological concept based on the rewards-punishment model. Operant conditioning, in particular, refers to the way good behavior can be strengthened when reinforcements or rewards follow after their occurrence.

Conversely, bad behavior can be controlled and diminished when punishment follows them immediately. However, this is an old school way of dog training and many professional trainers don't use this anymore, unless the dog's temperament makes it difficult to use R+ training.

3. Distractions and alternate behaviors

Another option for handling negative behavior of your Goldendoodle would be to distract him from his bad behavior or to teach him an alternate positive behavior instead.

For instance, if your dog gets excited, his tendency is to jump around. You can curb this possibly destructive behavior by teaching him to sit instead when he gets excited.

Again, use positive reinforcement to teach this alternate behavior. Use treats to make him obey, but this time, make him work for it by dangling the treat in front of him until he follows you. Only reward him after he's obeyed your orders.

Some basic things you always want to remember no matter what are:

• Always reinforce positive behavior to give them a clear idea of what's right

• Never hold a grudge against your puppy, because it will confuse him. He won't know what he's doing wrong beyond the initial punishment, and he'll even be unsure of what he did wrong in the first place, cancelling the positive effect of the initial punishment

• Never hit, beat, or scare your puppy

• Never send your puppy to its crate as a punishment. This has a negative effect on crate training, and causes separation anxiety. You always want your puppy's crate to be a happy place, because its where he has to spend a lot of time

• Always look for the reason your puppy is behaving a certain way

• Only punish your puppy when you catch him in the act. Otherwise you leave a lot of room for confusion, and your puppy taking the punishment for one act as a punishment for another. Some specific examples of this will be given along the way.

• Always be consistent in training your puppy. If for example your dog is coming to you when called is good enough for praise once, it should be good enough for praise always. Never forget to tell your puppy when he's been a good boy.

• Stay calm and consistent in your attitude as well.

• Reward your puppy when he is calm, not obnoxious. You would then be rewarding obnoxious behavior, such as opening the door to let him outside when he is jumping and being hyper.

Patience & Fun are the Key Ingredients

Training should never be stressful for your Goldendoodle. It should always be fun and enjoyable, incorporated in playtime. This is also why it isn't recommended to extend training beyond 10 minutes, especially for young pups.

When you're training your Goldendoodle, remember that you should never rush him to learn too many things right away. Start with only a few commands and tricks, and add more only after he's mastered the first few.

## POTTY TRAINING YOUR PUPPY

You'd think that potty-training your Goldendoodle would be easy, given their intelligence, but you'd be surprised—some owners report having difficulties with a stubborn Dood who doesn't seem to want to potty-train.

I'd say you should go slow with your dog's training, especially during the first few weeks. The entire house-training process can be pretty overwhelming for him, despite his supposed intelligence and quick pick-up.

When can I begin potty training my puppy?

The best time to start potty training according to experts is when he is between 12 weeks and 16 weeks old. During this period, he has control of his bladder. From my experience, I've learned that potty training works best with crate-training (to be discussed in the following section), although you can also choose other alternative house-training techniques to "room in" your puppy properly. The keys to potty-training your Goldendoodle are consistency and frequency. Puppies need to relieve themselves at least every hour (45 minutes is optimal.). Establish a potty-training routine. For example, when you take him out of his crate or sleeping area, use the same door to go outside. Lastly take him to the same spot on your lawn to relieve himself.

Your full attention is crucial during the potty-training period. You should ensure that your dog is under your watch at all times. Accidents happen, and the best is to be there to prevent most of them. If your Goldendoodle is having "accidents" in the same spot of the house, he might be getting potty-trained on that spot, so you need to change his routine immediately.

Watch for signs when your dog is preparing to relieve himself, including sniffing and circling around a certain spot. Accidents usually happen immediately after your puppy wakes up or after a meal. Some puppies also have a tendency to pee when they get too excited during playtime.

Teach your puppy the "potty" command by saying it repeatedly while the puppy is in its designated area. As soon as your puppy does the right 'thing', give it tremendous amounts of praise and treats to show that you appreciate the good behavior. This step is crucial, because it's positive reinforcement at its finest.

If your puppy has an Accident?

When your puppy has an accident (and it will) you'll want to catch it red handed, give a firm "no" and take it right to its designated area. If you don't catch your puppy in the act, don't punish it. Puppies don't think like people, and he or she will have no idea what you're mad about. Instead of thinking "I get punished when I poop in the house" your puppy will think, "I get punished when Mommy sees my poop. I should hide it".

The next thing you know you'll find the poop under your bed instead of out in the open. The only way to let your puppy know that it's doing something wrong is by correcting it as it's happening, not after the damage is done. You'll just have to bite the bullet and smile through those events, keeping a sharper eye out for next time.

The time period of potty training a Goldendoodles can take as long as four to six months, but it depends on your dog's temperament and personality. Bear in mind that smaller Goldendoodle types have higher metabolisms and smaller bladders therefore they require more frequent potty trips to the yard. During training don't worry if there are 'accidents'. Continue the potty-training program that includes taking the dog out when you observe the first signs. Eventually he'll learn.

Potty training steps:

According to experts at the beginning place your puppy into a den area such as a crate or in a room, or even on a leash. Gradually when your dog learns that he should go outside to potty, give him more freedom to roam around the house.

At the beginning you can follow the below steps:

- Follow a regular feeding schedule

- Take away his food between his meals.
- Supervise your dog at all times with no free access around the house. Your puppy must be taught the correct place to eliminate. All accidents inside a house are due to humans since they are not following the aforementioned tip.
- Take puppy for potty trips first thing in the morning. Then every 30 minutes to one hour.
- After meals, after he wakes up and last thing before you go to sleep make sure to take him outdoors to potty.
- Keeping your puppy on regular meal times rather than any time free-feeding, you will have a much easier time finding out when he/she is more likely to go potty outdoor.
- Always take him to the same designated area to do his business because his scent will trigger him to go.
- Till he is trained stay with him outside.
- Praise the puppy and treat whenever he eliminates outside or even walk with him around the neighborhood which is a nice reward.

Once trained, you won't need to put him out anymore. Your dog will initiate to go out on the yard by himself through the door. At first, he might ask you to open the door for him, but he'd also eventually get accustomed to using a pet door if you choose to install one.

# CRATE TRAINING

Crate training is one of the most effective techniques for housetraining Goldendoodles. Essentially, you just buy or build him a crate (or a small confined space) where he will sleep, eat, and drink water when he's not out for playtime.

The idea here is to confine your puppy inside that space for most of the time (except during training, playtime and exercise time). He can have some free time to roam the house later on, but for the first few weeks, you need to keep him here to help him establish his personal space.

Dogs have a natural instinct to keep their private space clean—which means they won't like to relieve themselves inside a space they consider their territory. Plus, in case of accidents, you confine most of the damage to that particular spot of the house.

You want your puppy's crate to be big enough for wiggle room. This means your puppy should be able to stand and walk around, however not enough space to soil in one area and stand and walk around in another.

# How to crate train your Gooldendoodle- Method 1

These steps will be used in conjunction with potty training, since it's designed for you to perform this training while the puppy is young.

First things first: Introducing the crate to your puppy. Many dogs love their crate and they are happily go inside to take a nap or rest.

But…

This cannot happen from the beginning of course. In case your dog has never being crated then you should start the training slowly. The whole procedure might take from few days to few weeks or months because each dog is different. If you don't want your dog to have negative feeling for the crate, then don't push him into it.

In contrast make this training as positive as possible by throwing a tasty treat into the crate. Your dog naturally will go into the crate to eat it. Repeat this trick many times and then go outside with your Goldendoodle for a long potty trip. Come back after half an hour and keep throwing treats inside the crate till your dog is going into the crate without any anxiety signs or fear.

Another useful tip is feeding his meal in the crate. Normally he will eat the food without any problems.

Once your dog goes happily in the crate then start throwing some chow toys and start closing the crate's door for some seconds. While he is in give a second treat through the wired door and at the same time praise your dog. After some seconds let him out. Repeat this exercise many times a day and gradually increase the amount of time you leave the crate's door open. Remember that whenever the door is close you should move away slowly for a while, till he feels comfortable staying in the crate.

When you reach the point that he can stay in the crate for several hours or he is taking a nap then you have reached your first success training stage. Moreover, it is a matter of crate your dog in a positive manner and have in mind that crate is making life easier for both dog and owner.

# How to crate train your Gooldendoodle- Method 2

1. Leave your puppy in the crate without leaving the house. Don't leave any sort of toy or entertainment in the crate. This training is to teach your puppy to self-soothe.

2. Leave the room and be very quiet (have a book on standby, this could take a while). If it cries, leave it until it calms down. This can take a very long time, even up to an hour or two. The key is to not let your puppy out any sooner than it's point of calm.

3. As soon as the puppy stops whining, go in and give it a great amount of praise, and take it out to potty. Be sure to use the same route to the potty area every time, so it knows what's coming and doesn't get confused.

4. Afterward, you'll want to put your puppy back in the crate and repeat the steps.

5. Do not punish your puppy for begging to be let out of the crate. It already feels terribly anxious to be left in the crate, and probably equally as upset that you're not letting it out. Instead, simply ignore the puppy to give it

time to learn how to self soothe, then praise it for self-soothing.

Your puppy should take less and less time to calm down every time you place it back in the crate until it simply doesn't beg. This kills two birds with one stone because you're also reinforcing not going potty in the crate, but rather outside.

You'll want to do this training regularly with your puppy. When you're not training, it's perfectly okay to give your puppy a toy to play with during crate time.

When your puppy gets better about not going potty in the crate, you'll want to be sure not to break the rule of not letting it out of the crate when it's whining on days when you come home from work and you find him anxious.

## How to crate train an older Goldendoodle dog

The most important thing about crate training an older or senior Goldendoodle is to avoid potty accidents and learn to eliminate in a certain potty area.

What you need to do?

Follow some simple steps:

First and foremost, rule is not to crate a dog more than he can 'hold it'. Every dog need time out to go potty, pee, exercise or play with their owners.

Very important…

If he is roaming free in the house his den-instinct will not work which means he might potty anywhere. Unfortunately, you need to stick on him and watch every move to identify body language signs that indicates he need to potty. Potty accidents might slow down the training and confuse him.

Stick on a schedule since dogs enjoy having routines such as meal time, play time sleep time e.t.c. Usually dogs enjoy crate however sometimes dogs need some extra time being with their loved ones before they go in the crate.

Make sure your Goldendoodle has plenty of free play time before crated. Create a routine that feeds better for your needs.

Important rule:

Never crate a dog more than 8 hours (max) on a period of one day. Keep in mind that even a trained old dog can have problems controlling his bladder for long period of time. Keeping a schedule will make the training easier:

**Morning** – as soon as your dog wakes up take him outside to pee or poop. Give your dog time to finish since not all dogs are the same. Then take him back to crate till you have breakfast.

**After breakfast** take him for a second round. Some exercise might help to poop faster. After he is done bring him indoor for some free time but watch him carefully for accidents. In case you notice the signs below take him outdoors for a potty break.

· He sniffing intensively

· Circling

· Sniffing behind the sofa or under the table.

**Middle-morning**: Let him outside to potty and then crate him by leaving a chew toy inside.

**After-lunch**: Potty break, together with some exercise or play. Take him for a small walk so that you keep his joints flexible. Then go indoors for some free time. You can let him in a pen close area to play with his toys. Remember to look for potty signs.

**Late-afternoon**: potty break then crate time or pen area

**Evening:** potty break, then give him his meal. After that one more time for potty break. Then it's up to you how you want to spent time with your dog. Just keep an eye on him…you know why.

**Before bed:** Most importantly take him for potty before sleep.

Most of adult dogs can hold it overnight, but some senior canines may need to potty during the night.

## Extra tips for crate training your Goldendoodle

- Leave a Kong toy filled with food in his crate before leaving from the house and let him enjoy it.

- Always take your dog to 'toilet' before putting him in the crate.
- Before you take him out from the crate wait for him to calm down and approach slowly to open the door.
- Another thing you can do is to leave in the crate an old T-shirt of yours that you had worn many days in a row. Your dog will be comfort by your smell.
- During the night you can cover the crate with a sheet while he sleeps. It seems to help your dog staying asleep longer.
- Play with your Goldendoodle outdoors before he goes to sleep to get him tired and loose energy. He will sleep faster.
- Lock the crate's door with food and his favorite toys. Don't open the door till he is really interested, and he wants to be inside the crate. This way the crate is the 'treat'. After he goes in the crate you can close it while he is eating. This method creates positive association with the crate!
- Place your dog's crate near you in another room so he can hear you talking or watching TV etc. It will help him to fall asleep.

# ESSENTIAL COMMANDS TO TEACH YOUR GOLDENDOODLE

## Sit

The most basic command and the easiest one. Make sure to start training with this one.

- Grab a treat and hold it close to your dog's nose. Then move the treat up. Naturally his head will follow the treat. This is causing him to sit. As soon as he sit say the command 'Sit' and give him the treat. Repeat until your Goldendoodle can sit without giving him a treat. Always ask your dog to sit before dinner or walks. Doing this he is more likely to learn this command faster.

## Come

Come is very useful command because you can call back your dog if he runs out of the front door or he is going to run after a cat.

- This exercise requires that the leash and collar in on your dog. Lower down your body and say 'Come' while you are slowly pulling the leash. As soon as he reaches you reward him with a treat and praise. When he comes without pulling the leash then practice without the leash until he masters this command.

## Down

This command can be challenging for you and your dog because this position is a submissive one. However with positive training you can succeed fast.

- Get a tasty treat and hold it in your fist. Hold your fist up to your puppy's nose to sniff it and then lower your hand towards the floor so he follows. Hold the treat in front of him to encourage his body to follow his head. When he is down say 'Down' and give him treat and lot of praise. In case your dog's body is not following the head give a gentle push on his back so he understands what you want from him. Repast this exercise till he can go down without a treat.

## Stay

Your dog should first learn the 'Sit' before you teach him the 'Stay' command.

- Say the command "Sit.". Open the palm of your hand in front of your dog's face and say 'Stay'. Move slowly backwards and reward him if he stays. Gradually increase the distance from your puppy before rewarding him.

This exercise can take longer since your dog needs to learn self-control especially with puppies and high energy dogs.

**Leave** it

This command is especially useful to stay out of trouble. Example when your dog sniffs something on the ground which is possibly dangerous

- Place one treat in each hand. And let him sniff the one with enclosed fist and say, "Leave it". Let him try to get the treat. As soon as he stops trying and gives you an eye contact, reward him by giving the treat from your other hand. Repeat till your Goldendoodle moves away from your hand when you say the command 'Leave it'.

These simple commands can keep your Goldendoodle safer and improve your relationship with him. Remember, that teaching these commands can be challenging but it's good investment of your time.

# SOCIALIZING YOUR GOLDENDOODLE PUPPY

Socialization is another important aspect for Goldendoodle training, especially if you want to minimize aggression tendencies. It's also vital if you have kids or other pets (especially if you have a cat as well) at home.

When your puppy arrives home, he needs time to get accustomed not only to his surroundings but also to the scent of his new owners. At four to six weeks of age, Goldendoodles will begin to fully explore and interact with their surroundings.

Introduce him to the family gradually. Allow him to interact freely with his surroundings and with your other pets if you have any. Just make sure that you take charge of the situation and intervene should there be any signs of fear, aggression, or anxiety from your puppy.

Socializing your Goldendoodle is way more fun than potty and crate training your Goldendoodle. This part involves a lot of playtime and compliments. You want to socialize your puppy so it doesn't turn into a miniature bully later in life, not allowing you to have guests or friends over, and not causing fights at the dog park. Like any other training, you'll want to take certain steps to make sure that your Goldendoodle is learning to be social the right way.

1. Take your Goldendoodle to the vet, and be sure it has all of the necessary vaccines. Be sure to let your vet know that you plan on socializing your puppy, because there are other shots required that aren't required for non-socialized dogs.

2. Start socializing your puppy as early as possible. If you get it incredibly young, you'll want to wait until it's at least 6 weeks old. Then it will be old enough to handle social situations.

3. Once it's old enough, you'll want to take your Goldendoodle out every day to experience a new place and new people.

4. Make a goal to introduce your puppy to 3 new people every day, and new dogs once or twice a week.

5. Be sure it has a lot of hands on interaction with people and dogs. Introducing your puppy to people doesn't mean someone speaks to the dog. Allow a new person to pet it, hold it or even walk it.

6.    Take your puppy in car trips, even if they're short ones.

7.    If your Goldendoodle is frightened, protect it, and simply tell people not to tough it if it growls or gets upset with a person or animal. It's better to do this than to let it feel abused.

8.    You want to introduce it to a diverse group of people. People that are all colors, ages, shapes and sizes, so you don't accidentally teach it a prejudice (it happens!).

9.    Take your puppy to a daycare and let all of the kids play all over it at least twice a week. You'll want to teach your puppy to be around kids, so it becomes desensitized to how rough and persistent children can accidentally be.

10.    Be sure to hand-feed your puppy once a day for the first 14 weeks so it doesn't become food aggressive.

11.    Also, for every bit of socialization training, you'll want this to last for the first 14 weeks. This is because this age is your puppy's critical period, which shapes the majority of its personality. This is when you'll need to be the most careful to instill the values you'll want it to have later.

Socializing your Goldendoodle is the best part of training, because it mainly involves letting your puppy socialize and play. You get to see how it reacts and interacts, which allows you to learn so much about its personality that you have yet to figure out. Have fun socializing your Goldendoodle! Allow him to be your buddy on your trips, and offer plenty of exercise as well!

# CHAPTER 4: DEALING WITH COMMON BEHAVIOR PROBLEMS

Even as a proud owner of Goldendoodles, I'd never say that these dogs are perfect. I love my dog and wouldn't trade him for anything else, but there are trying times when you can't help but get annoyed with some of his antics.

Goldendoodles become destructive when they get bored or when they are left to their own devices. Here are some ways you can deal with common behavioral issues of this dog breed. Of course, if any of these issues manifest early on in your puppy, you can handle them best by training them out of their behavioral issues.

## JUMPING

Jumping is a common behavioral problem not only with Goldendoodles, but a lot of family dogs with excessive energy levels. When you train him out of it, you need to establish yourself as the alpha dog that he needs to follow.

Also, don't make a habit of showering your dog with affection as soon as you walk inside the room. Giving them affection feels like a reward and excites them enough to jump at you. Because they think it's alright with you, they soon will do it to your guests too.

How you are responding to a jumbling Goldendoodle is very important.

For example:

While playing with his toy and he starts to jump then imminently stop playing and walk to another room ignoring him.

Another common 'jumping case scenario' is while you are preparing him dinner. If he starts to jump, then walk away with his food. Wait till he calms down. It helps if you give the command 'Sit' or 'Down'. As soon as he behaves then give him his meal.

When you come back from work and your Goldendoodle jumps on you then go outside close the door and wait till he calms down. When he is calmed then go inside the house again.

To deal with this problem your Goldendoodle needs to understand that jumping does not get him what he wants and makes the object they desire to go away.

As a result, your Goldendodle need to develop another way to get what he wants.

But…

When you observe that your dog for example, is sitting when you are preparing his food instead of jumping reward him heavily for it.

## BITING & NIPPING

Puppies naturally spend a lot of time chewing, investigating objects and playing. Their sharp teeth are involved in all these activities.

During playing with humans, puppies use their teeth and they often bite hands and chewing clothing. Biting seems cute to people when puppies are 7-8 weeks old however it's not nearly so pleasant when he is 3-4 months old.

Your goal is to train him to stop nipping and biting people. But, the most important goal is to teach him that humans have sensitive skin and must be gentle when using his mouth and teeth.

Your puppy must learn to control the force of his mouth and recognize the sensitivity of human skin. This is called 'bite inhibition'. Based on experts if a dog learned though his puppyhood life to use his mount gentle, then if he ever bites someone in a situation that he is afraid or has pain, he will be less likely to bite hart and break the human's skin.

A good real example of how puppies can learn to be gentle when biting is when they play with their brothers and sisters. When a group of puppies are playing together, you will see a lot of wrestling. During playing, puppies bite each other and sometimes hard. The victim will yelp and stop playing, so that the attacker understands that he was playing too hard.

## When do puppies stop biting and teething.

Part of housetraining your puppy is to find ways to stop the biting and mouthing behavior as well as stop chewing staff such as furniture or shoes. Like babies, puppies below six months old, will go through a period of teething. During teething period, puppies can be in a great pain so you need to understand that your puppy will bite often during this period of aging.

Puppies usually feel relief when they rub their gums on the object during chewing process. Another reason that puppies will chew your belongings is because they have your distinct smell that comforts the puppy. But, training your puppy not to chew things or biting you is easier than you think.

**11 ways to teach your puppy 'bite inhibition'.**

## 1. Keep your things away from the puppy

The first thing you must take into consideration is to keep your belongings away from the puppy when you are not with him. For your furniture, you can cover the chewing areas such as the shelf edges or sofa legs with some bad-tasting substance. To prevent the puppy from licking or chewing the furniture you can use pepper, or other products, such as bitter apple, bitter cherry. They are designed to prevent a puppy from licking or chewing them. Buy some soft dog chew toys, as the puppy will focus more on them instead on your skin and furniture.

Don't play aggressively with your puppy, like wrestling or chasing. If you play aggressively you will encourage him to start biting with excitement. Puppy will learn to associate biting and mothing with fun activities. Only after your puppy learns that biting is not a good behavior, you can start playing physical games with him.

## 2. High-pitched yelping sound

First step is to start playing with your dog. Let him mouth your hands till aggressive puppy biting starts. Then you should give a high-pitched yelping sound as if you are hurt and let your hand go limp. Usually this is enough to stop your puppy from biting.

If yelp did no help then you can use a loud, "Ow! When puppy stops mouthing you praise him, give him a treat and resume playing.

<u>Very important:</u> Don't repeat the limp and yelp process more than three times in a period of fifteen minutes. Whenever your cute fur ball behaves and does not bite, make sure you tell him some good pleasant words and pet him all over his boy.

## 3. Time out method: teach your dog that gentle play continues, but painful stops

If the above method doesn't work you can switch to Time – Out procedure which can be very effective. In this exercise, he will learn that gentle play continues, but painful play stops.

While playing with your dog wait till he starts mouthing you and remove your hand from his mouth. Ignore for 20 seconds. Stopping interaction with your dog can work perfectly most of the times. If he continues mouthing you then stand up and walk away to another room. As soon as your puppy is calm engage in appropriate play. Eventually your puppy will learn that, appropriate behavior results to getting your attention.

Repeat this method until your canine can play with your hands gently and you don't feel the pressure from his sharp teeth.

## 4. Using a chew toy can satisfy your puppy's urge to biting things.

Another good method is to remove your hand from his mouth before he starts to chew you and replace it with some dog chew toys. In this way your puppy's urge to mouth things will be satisfied.

Alternatively, you can distract him by giving him treats from your other hand so that you are teaching him getting used to being touched without mouthing.

## 5. Enroll your dog into a specialized training class

A good way to help your puppy to understand that mothing humans is not okay at all is to teach him to be obedient. You can enroll your puppy into a specialized training class where he can socialize with other puppies and will get a proper obedience training.

One important thing to keep in mind is that your dog cannot learn everything in one night therefore be patient since this is a slow process. By enrolling your dog into training classes you can rest assured that your canine will grow into a good and healthy dog.

## 6. Pinching the lips inward when puppy bites

In order to stop your puppy from biting, you can grab his lip and push it over his teeth. Pinching his lips inward around the puppy's own teeth end up biting his own lips. Eventually he will stop this bad habit.

## 7. Pinch or choke collar

For puppies around 6 months old using pinch or choke collar can be very effective. During play 'biting' time use a pinch or choke collar on your dog and every time he bites give the leash a short quick tug.

By this action/correction your puppy will develop an unpleasant sensation every time he starts biting. Sonner or later will stop this behavior in a short period of time.

Many dog trainers do not approve this method because it's a bit extreme. You could use this method only in rare extreme biting cases. Personally, I have never used this method since I didn't have to. It is wiser to educate your puppy instead of 'punishing' him.

## 8. Burn off his energy

Taking care, a puppy can be a lot of work. Sometimes you can think that their energy seems inexhaustible. They have the curiosity to investigate anything within their range. Burning off the energy will help your puppy to stop biting.

So, start burning off some puppy energy. Take him outdoors and play physical games like fetch. Some puppies can use up that energy by a simple walk while others need more activities to lose that energy such as long walks.

When you are done go back to the house and continue playing.

## 9. Teach your puppy to go to a specific place

Another way to prevent biting is to start teaching him to "go to bed" or "go to place". Once he can execute this command then use it when puppy starts biting you. Eventually he will learn that when misbehaved 'no play time'.

## 10. Put him to 'sit', 'down', heel or stay

Additionally, put your puppy on a sit, down, heel or stay position immediately after he starts biting. Teaching him these basic commands can be very useful. Keep your dog in any of the positions for 1-2 minutes. Hopefully your dog will learn that mouthing you, means 'loss of freedom'.

## 11. Teach him that biting never going to get him a treat

Before start playing with your dog have some tasty treats in your pockets. Once your puppy starts mouthing, turn your back and ignore him. Wait until he is calm, give him a tasty treat and praise him. Repeat as many times as needed so your puppy eventually stops biting. He will learn that biting and grabbing a hand is never going to get him a treat.

# DIGGING

So you prize your perfectly manicured lawn? Well, the bad news is that you've just added Goldendoodle to your family, one of the most naturally curious, explorer breeds you'd find.

While it might be tempting to punish your dog for ruining your backyard, that won't solve the digging problem. Basic solutions include trying to find ways to eliminate the boredom he must feel from time to time.

You can also use safe red flags to tell him that what he's doing is wrong and won't be tolerated. For example, you can train the garden hose on him while he's digging to startle him (though this approach might not work if your dog loves getting himself wet).

Here are a few additional tips to prevent your Goldendoodle from digging:

1.    Control the access your Goldendoodle has to digging holes. One of the simplest ways to do this is to supervise your puppy whenever it's in an area where he can dig.

2.    Remember that you must catch him in the act in order to correct the behavior.

3.    Have toys available to distract your Goldendoodle.

4.    Wait for him to start digging. He'll do it in front of you because he doesn't know that it's bad behavior, and thinks that nothing's wrong.

5.    Once you see him do it, tell him "stop digging" very firmly. When he stops, give him a treat and a toy to play with for distraction, and plenty of praise for good behavior.

6.    Catch your pup as many times as possible, so he learns what "stop digging" means.

7.    Once he understands the command, he'll do it behind your back. When you find a hole, you should be able to take him to the hole and say, "stop digging" and give him the distraction toy. When he takes the toy, praise him and tell him good boy. He'll remember what the command means, and know that it's still not right to dig even when you're not around.

If you want to give your puppy a place to dig, get a sandbox. Whenever you find him digging in the yard, use the sandbox in exchange for the toy. Just like potty training, you want to catch him in the act, tell him "no", and put him in the sandbox and tell him to "dig". Praise him for digging in the right spot.

## CHEWING

Every puppy chews. They chew your shoes, clothes, bed sheets and comforter, stuffed animals that don't belong to them, and just about anything else that fits comfortable in their mouth. It's one of the most destructive and frustrating behaviors to deal with, but it will likely happen to you.

Just like with biting, puppy time is the time to teach not to chew. When he doesn't have anyone else around and he's teething, he'll be looking for something to chew.

1.    Have fun chew toys for your puppy, and always keep them out and easily accessible for him.

2.    Introduce him to his toys. Don't just put the toy on the floor when you bring it home, put it directly into your Goldendoodle's possession.

3.   Supervise your pup at all times while he's free to roam. Watch him and wait for him to get ahold of anything he's not supposed to have, and quickly tell him "drop it". Once he drops it, give him one of the toys you've already put in his possession. This is communicating to your puppy that he's only allowed to chew on the things you give to him.

While the steps are easy, this involves consistency. You can only use this when you catch him in the act, not later. So be sure to have your puppy safely in his crate when you're not home, where he only has access to his toys. When he's out, feel free to set him up and test him, giving you more of an opportunity to deter his behavior.

Put a different item out every day close by his toy and see if he goes for it, and when he does, just follow the steps above to prevent him from becoming a habitual chewer.

## SEPARATION ANXIETY

Because Goldendoodles love their families so much, they tend to become extremely clingy to their owners. This often results in separation anxiety wherein they resort to destructive behavior when their owners leave them alone even for brief periods.

Although you can't make your dog not love you enough to miss you when you're not around, you can do something to make him comfortable and put him at ease. Consider the following options:

1.     Be careful not to reinforce your Goldendoodle's separation anxiety. This means no long goodbyes or happy hellos. Don't give him attention when he's acting up, or you'll be encouraging his behavior.

2.     Change your routine a bit from day to day. Leave earlier for work one day; make it home a little earlier or later the next. Start working night shift once a week, or simply take an evening stroll without your Goldendoodle to leave him home for a bit.

3.     Leave for small periods of time, at different times, daily. Your Dood will quickly see that you are coming back every time, and grow a little less anxious.

Reinforce good behavior always. Still, you need to ignore your puppy for the first 10 or so minutes after you arrive home each time, in order to keep the "long goodbyes" rule intact. After ignoring, if your puppy is still a good puppy, you'll want to show him some attention and praise him for being good.

## Puppy Separation Anxiety Solutions

Puppy's separation anxiety caused when your dog exhibits stress and/or behavioral problems and could be caused from the lack of exercise or activities. As a result, your puppy doesn't know how to deal with stress and he can get destructive.

Dogs are pack animals. They aren't used to being left alone. And when their humans go away, they resort to destructive behaviors in order to burn off the excess energy. Unfortunately, it is one of the most common reasons that owners give up on their canines.

This problem can be treated with just simple training steps which will be covered below.

## Possible Causes of Separation Anxiety

Main factors at this problem includes

- Genetics
- lack of socialization
- Dogs that lack confidence
- Due to over bonding,
- Under socialization,

- Lack of communication and training
- No knowledge of what is expected from them,
- Mistreatment in the past,
- Dogs that have been abandoned or rehomed have more chances to exhibit separation anxiety.

## How Can I Identify if My Dog Has Separation Anxiety?

Look out for one of these behaviors:

1. Your dog is chewing pillows or furniture even scratching at the door.
2. Barking or whining non stop
3. Urinating on the house floor.
4. Trying to escape from a room or crate
5. Extreme pacing and restlessness
6. Extreme salivation and panting
7. Drooling
8. Vomiting
9. Coprophagia
10. Dilated pupils
11. After coming home, your dog follows you everywhere in the house.
12. When you are preparing to leave he is whining or crying.

13. He doesn't eat his food.

## Most Common Case Study for Separation Anxiety

A main concern for a Goldendoodle owner is separation anxiety especially for those who work full time. This can be a serious issue for you and your goldendoodle, as well as affecting your neighborly relations. Howling and crying while you are away can be disturbing and annoying for your neighbor. This is the main reason that the first few days to make sure that your puppy get time alone.

It will be distressing to your puppy if you give him your full attention while you are home. Why? Because you don't want there to be a big difference from when you are home and when you are gone.

Therefore while you are home give him time in his own space whether it is in his crate or in his puppy space where he can play with his toys. Of course Goldendoodle puppy needs regular inspection during the day especially if you are potty training. Consider asking someone to look in on your dog periodically. Or even consider buying a dog monitor for some pet interaction even while you are away.

Model that dispenses treats, Music, white noise, nature sounds even Animal Planet on T.V. can help give your Goldendoodle some "company" so that he doesn't feel as if he has been completely abandoned.

## Tackle Separation Anxiety

Below are some tips for this problem so that you and your puppy can be calmer when you are apart.

## Exercise:

Just like humans exercise is the key to release some energy and stress. Go for a long walk with your dog or jogging.

The target is to make the dog tuckered so that he will be in a resting mode and sleep by the time you leave home.

## Play Games:

Another way to make your dog tired is to play games like fetch. 30 minutes of play time will get your dog tired just like a long walk. The more tired your dog gets the calmer he will be.

## Kong Toy

A very effective way to release the dog's stress is to use a stuffed Kong toy. Dogs love peanut butter. Give the Kong to your dog before you leave from home. The Kong will keep your dog busy for more than 30 minutes. By repeating this he will associate you leaving from home with getting a delicious treat. So it worth trying this technique and see how it gets.

## Removing triggering anxiety signs.

Your puppy sense when you are getting ready to leave house. How? When you pick up your keys, or put on your clothes or shoes your dog will get into the anxiety mood.

What to do?

Pick up your keys several times a day but don't leave the house. Instead act normal do what you are usually do. Or put on the shoes or the jacket and sit down to watch tv for half an hour. Hopefully the dog will not get triggered every time you are getting ready to leave home.

## Leave the house for 5 minutes

Leave the house for 5 to 10 minutes each time several times a day and then come back to the house. When you see that your dog is getting used to those short periods without any anxiety signs the increase the time gradually until you reach the desired result. Let's say if you work full time then your goal is to reach the period of 8 hours.

**Conclusion:**

To succeed you need to have patience. Training your dog to overcome anxiety could be very time consuming. Therefore, be ready to sacrifice your free time or rest time to train your fog. But…This is a small price to pay to have a healthy and well-adjusted puppy or dog.

## EXCESSIVE BARKING

You can't sleep because your dog is barking at night? Your neighbor is complaining about it?

If this is sound familiar keep reading. I will try to give you some techniques to assist you to stop your dog from excessive barking.

But don't expect to succeed over one night. Unfortunately, it will take longer time to teach your dog to stop barking if this is an old habit. There are many reasons why your dog is barking. However, some of the advices below may be required that you know the reason that your dog is barking.

Below are some tips before you start the training:

Don't scream at your Goldendoodle to make him stop. He will think that you are also barking.

Training sessions should be short.

You and your family should keep same training methods so your dog is not confuse.

**Training steps to stop barking**

1. Try finding what is triggering your dog to bark and remove it.
Your dog is not barking for no reason (ok sometimes when he/she is very bored). Some common reasons why dogs are barking are:

Humans or animals are passing by the street. If your dog is indoor close the curtains or take him to another room. If he is outdoor then take him inside the house.

2. Ignoring him while he is barking could make him stop since you are not giving him the attention that he craves. Your attention could only reward your dog and make        him        bark        even        more.

I know its hard but:

Don't speak

Don't touch

Don't look

After he stops barking even for some seconds it's the right time to reward him with a treat and then praise him. You have to be consistence and wait as long as it takes. For example if your dog barks for half hour and you cannot take it anymore and you start screaming at him then next the time he will bark it will be for an hour. This is because he learns that he continue barking until you pay attention to him. If your dog is in a restricted area such as crate or a crate room then:

Wait until he stops barking. Remember don't speak, Ddon't touch, Ddon't look. As soon as he stops barking praise him and give him a tasty treat. Slowly he will understand that being quite will get him a reward.

Try increasing the time that being quite before giving the treat. Start with 2 sec, 5 sec, 10 sec and so on.

3. During time your dog will get used to the objects or sounds that make him bark.

At the beginning place the 'thing' that makes him barks far away. In normally conditions he will not bark. Give him a treat. Then slowly bring the stimulation object closer and keep giving him treats. Lastly move the treat out of sight and stop feeding your dog. The bottom line of this exercise is to teach him that the stimulus object can lead to good tasty treats.

Training process:

Ask a friend who has a dog to stand out of sight so your dog won't bark. Ask your friend to come toward your dog and at the same time keep giving treats to your dog. Stop feeding him when your friend goes out of sight. Perform this exercise many times. Your dog might take days or even weeks to stop paying attention to the stimulus object.

4. Teaching your dog the 'quite command' can be very challenging. First step is to teach him to 'speak' on your command even if it sounds strange. Say the command 'speak,' and wait till he starts to bark. Then place a tread in front of his nose and wait till he stops and sniffs the treat. This is the right time to give him a treat.

Repeat this command many times during the day. As soon as he learns the command 'speak' its time to teach him the 'quite' command.

Find a place with no distraction maybe in your backyard or inside your house. Ask him to 'speak.' As soon as he barks say 'quiet' and put the treat in front of his nose with your hand closed. Give the treat and praise him for stop barking and being quite.

You can also ask a friend to ring the bell. Normally your dog will start barking towards the 'intruder'. Use the aforementioned way to make him quite. As soon as your dog learns the 'quite' command it is time to practice in places with more distractions such as your backyard.

5. Redirect his barking with something else. For example if someone is at the door toss a treat on

his bed. Normally he will go after the treat. At the same time open the door. Repeat this exercise until he remains on his bed. To make the exercise more difficult have your friend to ring the bell while your dog is on his                                                              bed.

6. Your dog has huge storage of energy especially when is a Goldendoodle. They need a lot of exercise to lose their energy. A tired dog barks less. Try making your dog tired by playing games or going for long walks with him.

# CHAPTER 5: HEALTH AND VETERINARY CARE

## DOG INSURANCE – DO YOU NEED IT?

Just like the human insurance, is going to vary. Different rates for different breeds and ages.

Many people would consider having a dog insurance, so they don't have to choose between a 4000 $ operation and a 40 $ shot to put down the dog because they cannot afford it.

Pet insurance covers the bills if your dog gets sick or injured based on what the policy covers. You may find that some insurance policies exclude cancer or hip dysplasia, but you can pay extra to add it to the policy. Some other companies' plans cover everything, as long as the disease or condition is not pre-existing.

Dog insurance does not cover services like spray or neuter, annual bloodwork, vaccines or dental cleanings, unless you are paying the extra add-on. Insurance for dogs make sense financially wisc if you have a new healthy puppy. Puppies insurance policies are the least expensive knowing how much trouble they can get into. So, in case your puppy is injured could make a policy worthwhile.

Older dogs are more expensive to insure. Financially wise it does not make sense to buy insurance for senior dog. As aforementioned any pre-existing health conditions will be excluded from the policy. Some dog companies might even decline to cover old dogs over a certain age.

## What Most Dog's insurance Cover

- Diagnostic tests.

- Operations

- Medications.

- Treatment.

## What Most Don't Cover

- Some dog insurances don't cover dental.

- Also, some of them don't cover preexisting or hereditary conditions.

So, dog insurance really "worth it"? The answer differs for each person and every dog. You might decide to have an insurance for your dog and never have to use it. However, a major medical condition can cost thousands of dollars.

# VETERINARY CARE

## 1. Vaccinations

Please consult a licensed VET professional before utilizing the information.

Puppies are given either a first and second set of vaccinations, or a first second and third set of vaccinations in the first weeks of their life. Whether they are given a set of two vaccinations or a set of three vaccinations is determined by the veterinary practice, and varies from one country to another. The types of vaccinations are standard though.

All puppies must be given their first vaccinations at between 6 to 8 weeks of age. The next vaccination will be at around 10 weeks of age, and if the vet works on a three-vaccination standard, the last vaccination will be three weeks later. After that all adult dogs must be vaccinated annually around the anniversary of their last vaccinations. The first puppy vaccination is a mild dose protection against:

- Bordetella Bronchiseptica - a highly contagious bacterial infection that causes severe coughing, vomiting, seizure and potentially death; it is the primary cause of what is commonly known as 'kennel cough' .

- Canine Distemper - a highly contagious viral infection that attacks the respiratory, gastrointestinal and nervous system of dogs. It causes discharge for the eyes and nose, fever, coughing, diarrhoea, vomiting, involuntary twitching, seizures, paralysis and often death. There is no treatment for Canine Distemper so early vaccination is essential.

- Canine Parainfluenza - a highly contagious viral infection that attacks the respiratory system and can lead to tracheobronchitis. It causes coughing, nasal discharge, fever, lethargy and loss of apetite.

The second round of puppy vaccinations are stronger and are commonly referred to as DHPP. If this is to be the final puppy vaccination for the next year, it will be increased to include, Bordetella, Coronavirus, Leptospirosis, Lyme Disease and Rabies. DHPP includes:

- Distemper

• Hepatitis (Adenovirus) - a highly contagious viral infection that attacks the eyes, liver, lungs, kidney and spleen, causing abdominal pain and swelling, fever, congestion, jaundice and vomiting. It can be fatal, and there is no cure. Early vaccination is essential; it is unrelated to Hepatitis in humans.

• Parainfluenza

• Parvovirus - a highly contagious viral infection that attacks the gastrointestinal system causing fever, loss of appetite, vomiting and bloody diarrhea. Young puppies under 4 months of age are particularly susceptible and they can die within 48 hours due to extreme dehydration. Older dogs are also susceptible, and it can be fatal as there is no cure. Early vaccination is essential.

Additional vaccinations that could be included offer protection against:

• Coronavirus - a viral infection that attacks the gastrointestinal system and occasionally the respiratory system as well. It causes loss of appetite, nausea, vomiting and diarrhea. There is no cure and it can be fatal. Early vaccination is essential.

• Leptospirosis - a bacterial infection that causes loss of appetite, fever, vomiting, diarrhea, jaundice, muscle stiffness and pain, kidney failure and liver failure. It can be treated with antibiotics if diagnosed quickly. It is transmittable to humans.

• Lyme Disease - also known as Borreliosis, it is an infectious tick-borne disease caused by a bacteria called Spirochete. Initial symptoms include loss of appetite, fever, limping and swollen lymph nodes. Left untreated the disease can affect the heart, kidneys, liver, joints and have serious neurological complications. If diagnosed quickly it can be successfully treated with antibiotics, but relapse can occur.

• Rabies - a viral infection that invades the central nervous system causing anxiety, headaches, hallucinations, excessive drooling, paralysis and potentially death. It is most commonly spread through the bite of an infected animal. Without a quick diagnosis, it is almost always fatal. Early vaccination is essential. Rabies is transmittable to humans.

If a third round of vaccinations is given, it is usually a repeat of the DHPP vaccinations. Some vets prefer to include some of the above-mentioned vaccines with the third round of vaccinations rather than with the second.

## 2.    Internal Parasites

Worms are the most common internal parasites found in dogs. Most puppies are born with intestinal Round Worms transmitted from their mother through lactation. Deworming is essential from a very young age. The most common worms found in dogs include:

•        Heart Worm – are spread by mosquitoes and contamination is preventable with regular prophylactic medication. Larvae lodge in the right side of the heart from where they can spread to other organs causing injury and blockage. There are no early symptoms, but severe infestation causes fatigue, lethargy, loss of appetite, breathing difficulties and ultimately organ failure.

•        Round Worms - are often transmitted through lactation when larvae pass from mother to pup. Round worm larvae can also be transmitted from mother to pup in-utero from the mother's tissue. They infest the puppies' intestinal tract. If left untreated they can cause emaciation and ultimately death through intestinal blockage

• Hook Worms - are often transmitted through lactation on in-utero. They migrate to the small-intestine and latch on the walls to feed off blood. If left untreated they can easily kill small puppies by causing severe anaemia from blood loss. In older dogs, they cause emaciation, lethargy and a compromised immune system that can make the dog susceptible to other illness as a result of anaemia.

• Tape Worms - are transmitted to dogs by fleas. They latch themselves to the walls of the digestive tract and feed off the stomach contents. If left untreated they can cause emaciation and starvation. Over-the-counter generic medicines will not kill them: the infestation must be treated by a vet.

• Whip Worms - lodge themselves in the first section of the large- intestine and feed off the stomach contents. They can cause emaciation and starvation. They are difficult to detect, and infestations must be treated by a vet.

All worms discussed above except Heart Worm are passed on to adult dogs through feces of an infected cat or dog. The feces contain larvae and eggs, and these are ingested by puppies and adult dogs from the ground around the faces or by ingestion of the faces.

Puppies are dewormed for the first time at the same time that they are vaccinated for the first time. Some breeders will start de-worming small puppies from 2 weeks of age and every second week after that until they are 12 weeks old because many puppies are born with worms.

After their last round of vaccinations or last puppy de-worming, all puppies and dogs should be de-wormed every three months for the rest of their life.

## 3.   External Parasites

If your Goldendoodle is a household pet that lives indoors, you must take preventative treatment for internal and external parasites. A well cared for dog that is groomed regularly should not have many parasitic infestations. If an infestation is identified and treated immediately, it will clear very rapidly. The most common parasites that your Goldendoodle will encounter include:

•      Fleas - that will most likely be picked up when going for walks (particularly in parks and in the country-side) or from over-night kennels and grooming parlours. Fleas crawl along a dog's coat onto the skin and suck blood through the skin. They will be immediately visible if you brush your Goldendoodle regularly. Symptoms are constant scratching and inflamed skin. Some dogs have an allergy to flea bites and that can cause dermatitis.

There are many treatments for flea infestations that include sprays, shampoos and dips. Prevention is the best option and quality sprays that are regularly sprayed into your Goldendoodle's coat and around your house are the best deterrent.

• Ticks - are picked up from grassy areas and bushes. They detect their host from body heat and on contact crawl through the coat and burrow into an area of skin to feed off blood. Ticks are clearly visible if you brush your Goldendoodle regularly.

There are topical treatments available that repel ticks and ticks can also be removed with a special device available from pet product retailers. Once a tick is removed and killed, no further treatment is necessary.

Ticks can spread a variety of serious disease that varies from country to country and on the type of tick. If your Goldendoodle displays any sign of illness after you have found a tick on it, take it to your vet immediately and advise the vet that you removed a tick or ticks. Also, show the vet where on your Goldendoodles body each tick was removed.

• Mosquitoes - are flying insects that draw blood from its hosts' skin. In some countries, mosquitoes spread Heart Worm. Mosquitoes are prevalent in the warmer months of the year and proliferate around areas where there is stagnant water.

It is difficult to prevent your Goldendoodle from being bitten by mosquitoes, but some topical treatments that contain the ingredient Imidacloprid for repelling fleas and ticks also do repel mosquitoes.

• Lice and Mites - are both tiny parasites that burrow into the flesh and feed off blood. There are many different types of mites in particular.

If your Goldendoodle is an indoor dog that is a part of your household and family, it is most likely that you are keeping it well groomed and using quality external parasite repellents.

The only time your Goldendoodle might have an infestation of lice or mites is when you first bring it home as a puppy, and you bought it from a pet store or an online advert. Lice and mites spread rapidly in unhygienic conditions.

You will immediately see that your new Goldendoodle puppy's coat is dry or matted and that the skin is inflamed and flaky. Take your new puppy to your vet as soon as possible to get the right treatment to get rid of the infestation.

If you have kept the puppy in a dog bed or allowed it onto your carpets and furniture, ask your vet what you must use on these items because lice and mites are tiny, prolific breeders and their eggs are very robust. Lice and mites spread easily to other pets, and some can spread to humans as well.

## 4. Common Health Issues of Goldendoodles

If you bought your Goldendoodle puppy from a pet store or online advert you will not know if it has any genetic predisposition to certain health conditions.

Even though Goldendoodles are considered to be healthier than other breeds they do have some health issues. Some if the problems are the same as those of the pure breed heritages of the Poodle and the Golden Retriever dog. Most common issues are shown below.

## Diseases and Conditions Documented in Goldendoodle Dogs include:

• Allergic dermatitis or Atopy is an itchy skin problem (disease) which is caused by an allergy to different environment particles.

• Cataracts is a disease which affect the eye vision.

• Corneal Dystrophy a disorder which affects the eyes.

• Cranial cruciate ligament rupture is a rupture of a ligament in the knee which is causing pain and lameness to the Goldendoodle.

• Degenerative myelopathy is affecting the use of the rear legs and is a progressive degenerative disease of the spinal cord

• Diabetes mellitus: Liver produce insufficient amounts of insulin production.

• Distichiasis is when extra eyelashes grows from glands of lower eyelid the upper.
• Some poodles and poodle mixes may react to Drug "Glucocorticoids" which may cause local hair loss.

• Ectopic Ureter can cause lack of voluntary control over urination. Is created from an abnormal routing of the tube which carries urine from the kidney to the bladder

• Elbow dysplasia affects the process of developing of certain parts of the elbow joint during the growing phase of your dog's life.

• Entropion causes the eyelid to rotate forcing the eye lashes to rub the cornea

• Epilepsy is a seizure disorder which can occur in certain ages (between 2 to 5 years).

• Food Allergy caused by different food ingredients and affects dog's skin development.

• Gastric torsion is a disease related to stomach filling with air and twisting and it is a life-threatening illness.

• Glaucoma is an eye disease where the pressure within the eye increases.

• Hemangiosarcoma is a cancer which affects the spleen, heart or liver.

• Hip dysplasia causes pain to hip joint which results to pain, lameness and arthritis.

• Hyperadrenocorticism is a disorder which is affecting the adrenal glands producing excessive cortisol, resulting in illness.

• Hypertrophic Osteodystrophy (HOD) – is a disease which causes lameness due to bone inflammation.
• Hypoadrenocorticism (Addison's Disease) – is causing a deficiency of steroid production.

• Hypothyroidism causes illness and results when the thyroid gland does not function properly.

• Immune-mediated hemolytic anemia – is causing destruction of red blood cells and is an immune disorder.

• Insulinoma is causing hypoglycemia and is a malignant tumor of the pancreas that produces excessive amounts of insulin.

• Interdigital Dermatitis affecting the feet and nails and is also known as pododermatitis,

• Intervertebral Disk Disease can cause paralysis. It is a disorder that affects spinal disks which eventually causes pain and difficulty walking.

• Hemophilia is disease which results in excessive bleeding.

• Laryngeal Paralysis can cause paralyzed creating noisy difficult air flow into the trachea and is a disorder of the laryngx.

•Limbal Melanoma is a cancer of the eyes.

• Lipomas are fatty tumor of the subcutaneous tissue.

• Lymphosarcoma (lymphoma) is malignant cancer related to the lymphoid system.

• Myasthenia gravis is a disease that affects the muscles causing them to be weak.

• Patellar luxation is a disorder of the kneecap placement.

• Perianal Fistula infection is affecting the anal glands and tissues around the anal area.

• Progressive Retinal Degeneration can lead to blindness and is caused by nerve cells at the back of the eye which they degenerate.

• Squamous Cell Carcinoma is a skin cancer.

• Other diseases found usually in goldens than in other breeds are osteochondrosis, seborrhea, hot spots, diabetes and hypothyroidism

## CONCLUSION

A Goldendoodle is a wonderful addition to any home, as long as you have the space and the time to offer the same amount of love and attention that your Goldendoodle will shower you with. If you've already brought a Goldendoodle home, you probably already know all of the great qualities your dog possesses. Not every pet experience is the same, and though there are many cases of a Goldendoodle being the ideal family pet, there is always the possibility that you will face some issues. If you are struggling with housebreaking, or training your dog, seek the assistance of a professional trainer. Even when it seems as if you simply can't form a bond, or have a successful relationship with your dog, a good dose of training may work miracles. As excited as you are to have a new pet, your new pet is just as excited, so be patient, use a positive attitude, and enjoy! Remember that when you decide to bring a Goldendoodle into your family, you are going to have a pet that will adore you with all of their being, that deserves to be treated in the same way. With such a laid back personality and generally good health a Goldendoodle a great choice for your next pet.

Good luck with your new puppy!

'Thanks for reading. I hope you found this book useful. If you did enjoy the book, please could you leave a review on the website where you bought the book.'